Making New Discoveries

BIBLE STUDY GUIDE

From the Bible-teaching ministry of

Charles R. Swindoll

INSIGHT FOR LIVING

Chuck graduated in 1963 from Dallas Theological Seminary, where he now serves as the school's fourth president, helping to prepare a new generation of men and women for the ministry. Chuck has served in pastorates in three states: Massachusetts, Texas, and California, including almost twenty-three years at the First Evangelical Free Church in Fullerton, California. His sermon messages have been aired over radio since 1979 as the *Insight for Living* broadcast. A best-selling author, Chuck has written numerous books and booklets on many subjects.

Based on the outlines and transcripts of Chuck's sermons, the study guide text is co-authored by Gary Matlack, a graduate of Texas Tech University and Dallas Theological Seminary. He also wrote the Living Insights sections.

Editor in Chief:
Cynthia Swindoll

Coauthor of Text:
Gary Matlack

Assistant Editor:
Wendy Peterson

Copy Editors:
Tom Kimber
Karene Wells

Text Designer:
Gary Lett

Publishing System Specialists:
Bob Haskins
Alex Pasieka

Cover Designer:
Nina Paris

Director, Communications and Marketing Division:
Deedee Snyder

Marketing Manager:
Alene Cooper

Project Coordinator:
Colette Muse

Production Manager:
John Norton

Printer:
Sinclair Printing Company

Unless otherwise identified, all Scripture references are from the New American Standard Bible, © The Lockman Foundation 1960, 1962, 1963, 1968, 1971, 1972, 1973, 1975, 1977. Used by permission. Scripture taken from the Holy Bible, New International Version, © 1973, 1978, 1984 International Bible Society, used by permission of Zondervan Bible Publishers.

An effort has been made to locate sources and obtain permission where necessary for the quotations used in this book. In the event of any unintentional omission, a modification will gladly be incorporated in future printings.

ISBN 0-8499-8630-3
COVER PHOTOGRAPH: The Stock Market
COVER ART: *Opere di Galileo Galilei*. Taken from Colin A. Ronan, *Galileo* (London: Weidenfeld and Nicolson, n.d.).
Printed in the United States of America

CONTENTS

INTRODUCTION

Can you imagine the thrill of being the first person to peer into space through a telescope? Or stand on the surface of the moon? Suppose you just discovered the cure for polio. Or heard another voice for the first time over a tiny wire. We could fill several pages with such exhilarating historical discoveries.

Discoveries, however, aren't limited to ancient days, scientific experiments, or technological breakthroughs. Every day we live, there are new things to be seen, new techniques to be learned, new insights to be realized. And when those new discoveries are related to the truths God has preserved for us in His Word, the joy we experience is often "off the chart." I know. I have had it happen to me more times than I can number.

That's what this study is all about—experiencing the joy of new discoveries in six specific areas of life. Marriage, friendship, work, worship, adversity, and evangelism—all six are vitally linked to our relationship with each other and with Christ, our Lord.

So unpack that old telescope and set it up. But instead of aiming it toward space, point it at the Scriptures. You just might see something you've never seen before—something that could change your life and enrich your relationships with others.

Chuck Swindoll

Chuck Swindoll

PUTTING TRUTH INTO ACTION

K nowledge apart from application falls short of God's desire for His children. He wants us to apply what we learn so that we will change and grow. This study guide was prepared with these goals in mind. As you go through the following pages, we hope your desire to discover biblical truth will grow as your understanding of God's Word increases and that you will be encouraged to apply what you've learned.

To assist you in your study, we've included a section called **Living Insights** at the end of each lesson. These exercises will challenge you to study further and to think of specific ways to put your discoveries into action.

On occasion a lesson is followed by a **Digging Deeper** section, which gives you additional information and resources to probe further into some issues raised in that lesson.

There are many ways to use this guide—in personal devotions, group studies, discussions with friends and family, and Sunday school classes. And, of course, it's an ideal study aid when you're listening to its corresponding *Insight for Living* radio series.

To benefit most from this study guide, we would encourage you to consider it a spiritual journal. That's why we've included space in the **Living Insights** for recording your thoughts and discoveries. We hope you'll return to those sections often for review and encouragement as you continue to grow in your walk with Christ.

Gary Matlack
Coauthor of Text
Author of Living Insights

Making New Discoveries

Chapter 1

DISCOVERING HOW TO MAKE A MARRIAGE WORK

Genesis 2:24–25; Proverbs 24:3–4

Do you ever bug your spouse to take one of those "Test Your Marriage" quizzes in magazines? Well, there's a much simpler way to gauge your marriage—all you need to do is observe one foolproof indicator: the common cold.

> The first year the husband says, "Sugar, I'm worried about my little baby girl. You've got a bad sniffle. I want to put you in the hospital for a complete checkup. I know the food is lousy, but I've arranged for your meals to be sent up from Rossini's. It's all arranged."
>
> The second year: "Listen, honey, I don't like the sound of that cough. I've called Dr. Miller and he's going to rush right over. Now will you go to bed like a good girl just for me, please?"
>
> Third year: "Maybe you'd better lie down, honey. Nothing like a little rest if you're feeling bad. I'll bring you something to eat. Have we got any soup in the house?"
>
> Fourth year: "Look, dear. Be sensible. After you've fed the kids and washed the dishes you'd better hit the sack."
>
> Fifth year: "Why don't you take a couple of aspirin?"

This chapter has been adapted from chapters 1, 3, and 7 of the study guide *Strike the Original Match*, coauthored by Lee Hough, from the Bible-teaching ministry of Charles R. Swindoll (Anaheim, Calif.: Insight for Living, 1992).

Sixth year: "If you'd just gargle or something instead of sitting around barking like a seal."
Seventh year: "For heaven's sake, stop sneezing. What are you trying to do, give me pneumonia?"[1]

Once the apple of his eye, you're now the seed between his teeth. She's gone from whispering "Snooky-ookums" in your ear to shouting, "Hey, get off the couch and help me with the dishes!" What happened?

Too often in marriages, affirmation and acceptance dwindle into insults and irritation. Though imperceptible at first, this kind of deterioration can eventually crumble a marriage. As J. Allan Petersen says, "Marriage is not wrecked by a blowout but rather by a slow leak—continued negligence and inattention."[2]

What can we do, then, to keep our marriages in good repair? Perhaps we could start with the *opposite* of the "blowout" formula: continued effort and attention.

Let's face it—successful marriages are built; they don't just happen. They require commitment and hard work—whether the project involves smoothing over a sharp, critical spirit, renovating a romance, or reinforcing the spiritual foundation. Hard work, yes, but not impossible.

Every building (or rebuilding) project starts with a set of blueprints, and the same is true of marriage. Our blueprint, God's Word, will help us know just where to build the walls . . . and where to knock them down.

God's Blueprint for a Strong Marriage

God's master plan for building a strong marriage begins "in the beginning"—with Creation itself.

Creation under Construction

In Genesis 1, we find a world under construction. Several times during the project, God steps back and surveys His work like a proud craftsman. He observes the light that now warms the planet. He watches the sea foam and curl in to the shoreline. He sizes up

---

1. Art Sueltz, as told by Bruce Larson in *The One and Only You* (Waco, Tex.: Word Books, Publisher, 1974), p. 20.

2. J. Allan Petersen, "Partnership before Parenthood," in *The Marriage Affair*, comp. and ed. J. Allan Petersen (Wheaton, Ill.: Tyndale House Publishers, 1971), p. 126.

the lush plants blanketing the earth and delights in the trees dripping with fruit. At every stage, God sees that it is "good" (vv. 4, 10, 12, 18, 21, 25). After creating man and woman, in fact, He concludes that His creation is "very good" (v. 31).

At one point, however, something is *not* good—the aloneness of the man.

> Then the Lord God said, "It is not good for the man to be alone." (2:18a)

The arrangement of the Hebrew words emphasizes the negative: "Not good to be the man alone."[3] Adam is isolated, incomplete. So God fashions a "helper suitable for him"—He creates woman (vv. 18b, 21–22).

Adam's response?

> "This is now bone of my bones,
> And flesh of my flesh;
> She shall be called Woman,
> Because she was taken out of Man." (v. 23)

The English doesn't quite capture the excitement of the moment. Remember, this is Adam's first glimpse of another human. We might paraphrase his reaction, "At long last! A gift from God to take away my aloneness!"

It's a joyful wedding—not only for Adam and Eve, but also for us. Because in their relationship, we find a plan for building strong marriages today.

Marriage God's Way

Let's look at the last two verses of Genesis 2, where God unrolls His blueprint for marriage in the form of four relational principles. First, we find the principle of *severance*.

> For this cause a man shall leave his father and his mother. (v. 24a)

Marriage works best when both partners separate themselves physically and emotionally from their parents to start a new life. This doesn't mean that parents and children should not be involved

---

3. John R. Kohlenberger III, *The Interlinear NIV Hebrew-English Old Testament* (Grand Rapids, Mich.: Zondervan Publishing House, Academic and Professional Books, 1987), p. 5.

in each other's lives. It does mean, though, that the husband and wife should focus their attention on establishing their own home and family. For parents, severance means turning their children loose—still being available for advice and guidance but allowing space for the couple to develop into a family of their own.

The next principle is *permanence*.

. . . and shall cleave to his wife. (v. 24b)

The Hebrew word for *cleave* means to "cling" or "stick to."[4] God designed marriage as a permanent relationship, a secure, unbreakable bond. The biblical motto for marriage isn't "Walk out if you can't work it out." It's "Cleave, don't leave." Divorce may seem like the easy way out. But broken bonds hurt deeply . . . and mend slowly.

Strong marriages also demonstrate *unity*, the third principle.

And they shall become one flesh. (v. 24c)

Unity starts with acceptance—realizing that God has provided a spouse who has strengths, weaknesses, abilities, interests, and perspectives unique to him or her . . . and different from us. The more each spouse lovingly affirms the other and appreciates his or her uniqueness, the more the two will operate as one.

Finally, a strong marriage requires *intimacy*.

And the man and his wife were both naked and were not ashamed. (v. 25)

In Hebrew, the word *naked* goes beyond physical exposure. It also suggests "that no barrier of any kind drove a wedge between Adam and Eve."[5] They had no secrets, no hidden agendas, no buried bitterness. Complete trust and transparency characterized their relationship.

Adam and Eve had the only ideal marriage—until they sinned. After disobeying God, their unhindered communion with Him and each other came to an end. Then they struggled, as have all married couples since, to rebuild their relationship according to God's design.

4. Earl S. Kalland, in *Theological Wordbook of the Old Testament*, ed. R. Laird Harris, Gleason L. Archer, Jr., Bruce K. Waltke (Chicago, Ill.: Moody Press, 1980), vol. 1, p. 177.

5. Victor P. Hamilton, *The Book of Genesis: Chapters 1–17*, The New International Commentary on the Old Testament Series (Grand Rapids, Mich.: William B. Eerdmans Publishing Co., 1990), p. 181.

Remodeling a Marriage

What can we do to repair the damage caused by sin and restore the harmony God intended? Proverbs gives us some practical guidelines and the right tools for remodeling a marriage.

Not beyond Repair

By wisdom a house is built,
And by understanding it is established;
And by knowledge the rooms are filled
With all precious and pleasant riches.
(Prov. 24:3–4)

Three verbs in this passage describe the process of remodeling. Notice the first—a house is *built*. The Hebrew word here is the same one used by Nehemiah to describe the rebuilding of the wall around Jerusalem (see Neh. 2:18). How encouraging! This shows us that a deteriorating marriage, like a fallen wall, need not be condemned; instead, with wisdom, it can be rebuilt.

The next verb, *establish*, means to "put right, correct."[6] With understanding, the home is set in order, made right, stabilized. What might have been tottering is now firm; it is built to last.

Notice, too, that by knowledge the house is *filled*. Filled with what? "All precious and pleasant riches." Solomon's not talking about a new mahogany dining table, a brass bed frame, or matching drapes and sofa set. Lovely as these are, they can't fill an empty heart. No, the riches he speaks of flow out of loving relationships, lives richly shared and remembered.

A household, then, that is not presently all it could be *can* be restored and made to flourish, stabilized and set aright, overflowing with fulfillment. Here's hope to hang on to!

The Right Equipment

Now that we have the guidelines for rebuilding a shaky marriage into a strong one, let's make sure we reach for the right equipment. The first thing we need is *wisdom* (Prov. 24:3a)—seeing with discernment. This is a God-given awareness of the value the Lord places on us and on our spouse. It's also seeking His perspective on

---

6. *The New Brown-Driver-Briggs-Gesenius Hebrew and English Lexicon*, Francis Brown, S. R. Driver, Charles A. Briggs (Peabody, Mass.: Hendrickson Publishers, 1979), p. 465.

5

our problems and differences. With wisdom's eyes, we can be more fair and less self-righteous because we'll recognize our spouse's dignity as a fellow child of God.

Next, we need *understanding* (v. 3b)—responding with insight. Once we begin to see with God's perspective, our hearts are more open to His ways of relating. When we're wrong, we'll admit it and act to put things right. When our spouse's inappropriate outburst catches us by surprise, we won't retaliate but patiently try to uncover the real cause. We'll be more attuned to treating others the way we want to be treated. Understanding enables us to see beyond life's surface irritations with a depth of insight that allows a mature, constructive response.

Finally, we need *knowledge* (v. 4a)—learning with perception. This is more than merely accumulating information. It means having a teachable spirit, a willingness to learn. In a marriage that's alive, we'll regularly make new discoveries about our mate, ourself, our home, our God. And we'll continually grow in our ability to value what really matters in life.

True, there's no such thing as a perfect marriage, since there are no perfect people. But we have a perfect God who gave us His perfect Word to live by. And He specializes in remodeling. Maybe we should stop trying to wing it . . . and read the instructions.

 Living Insights

He plugs in the Christmas lights . . . and almost electrocutes himself. He flips the switch to demonstrate the newly installed vacuum system . . . which slurps up the psychology paper his wife stayed up all night to finish. He throws his truck into reverse . . . and demolishes a freshly renovated front porch.

He's Tim "The Tool Man" Taylor of the television show *Home Improvement*, the most accident-prone handyman on the planet. He never reads the instructions, always acts before he thinks, and ruins almost everything he tries to fix.

Trying to build a strong marriage sometimes makes us feel like Tim "The Tool Man," doesn't it? Things don't work like they're supposed to. Everything we try goes up in smoke. And we wonder if we'll ever get it right.

That's when we need to remember that we're not building our marriages alone. God not only supplied His blueprint in the Scriptures,

He's right there with us on the project. Motivating and energizing us. Forgiving our mistakes. Touching up our shoddy workmanship. Hammering away while we sleep.

How much are you depending on God for your marriage? Do you regularly consult His blueprint and talk to Him in prayer? Does He wear the foreman's hat? Maybe you need some encouragement that He's still involved and still cares about the success of your marriage.

Read the following passages, and write down what they suggest about God's interest and involvement in your marriage.

Psalm 42:5, 8 _____

_____

_____

_____

Psalm 127:1–2 _____ .

_____

_____

_____

John 15:4–5 _____

_____

_____

_____

By all means, keep on building! Improve. Reinforce. Remodel. And remember, you're not alone. Your marriage is in the hands of the world's only perfect Carpenter.

 Living Insights STUDY TWO

Remember the four principles given in Genesis 2?

- Severance—shifting physically and emotionally from parents to partner

- Permanence—commitment to stay bonded together
- Unity—working as one, appreciating one another's differences
- Intimacy—physical, emotional, and spiritual openness

Which of these four qualities would you and your spouse say needs the most work in your marriage? Is overdependence on parents keeping your relationship from growing? Is the glue that once held you together starting to weaken? Do you find yourselves working against, instead of with, each other? How close are you letting your mate get to you?

Choose one principle that needs strengthening. Brainstorm with your mate about how to make improvements. Write down your ideas, and implement one of them over the next week or so. This kind of evaluation on a regular basis can do wonders for a marriage.

Principle on which to focus:_____

_____

Ideas for action:_____

_____

_____

_____

_____

_____

_____

_____

_____

Chapter 2

DISCOVERING THE VALUE OF DEEP FRIENDSHIPS

Ecclesiastes 4:9–12; John 15:12–17

April 29, 1992. If ever Takao Hirata needed a friend, it was on that day.

The intersection of Florence and Normandie in south-central Los Angeles no longer resembled a city street. The announcement of the Rodney King verdict had transformed it into a swirling vortex of hate and revenge. And Hirata's brown Ford Bronco was being sucked into its violent center.

There was no escape. As Hirata tried to lock the doors, a metal rod shattered his driver's-side window. A bottle flew through the opening and slammed against his skull. Then blows came in rapid fire from every direction. And they kept coming, even after the Japanese-American was unconscious—slumped over the steering wheel like a discarded doll.

That's when Gregory Alan-Williams moved in. An African-American, he blended with the mob. He shouldered his way through the crowd, urging those jockeying for a shot at Hirata to back off. Somehow, amid the bombardment of bottles and anti-Asian slurs, Alan-Williams managed to pull the bloody stranger from his Bronco and get him to the hospital.

Later on, during his rehabilitation, Hirata expressed his appreciation by giving a miniature samurai helmet to his rescuer and new friend. "You are my samurai," he said to Alan-Williams.[1]

Sometimes two people are better than one, especially when one is defenseless. Which is why friends are so important—they are there for us when we need them most. They don't always intervene in such a heroic manner; often, they serve in quiet consistency, helping in ways that seldom make the evening news. But they are no less important to us than Gregory Alan-Williams was to Takao Hirata.

Do you have a friend like that? Perhaps you can name several. Or perhaps you're feeling friendless right now. The Scriptures tell

---

1. Adapted from Gregory Alan-Williams' "You Are My Samurai," condensed from A Gathering of Heroes in Reader's Digest, March 1995, pp. 17–22. Samurai were noble warriors in feudal Japan who lived by an honorable code of ethics encompassing courage, loyalty, and sacrifice.

us that we can't make it alone; we need friends. And the first step to making new friends, as well as appreciating the ones we have, is seeing how valuable friendship really is.

Three Reasons Why We Need Friends

Looking back on a life of empty materialism, Solomon probably longed for the true treasure of friendship. In his pensive journal, Ecclesiastes, he gives us three reasons why "two are better than one."

A Friend Gives Encouragement When We're Weak

> Two are better than one because they have a good return for their labor. For if either of them falls, the one will lift up his companion. But woe to the one who falls when there is not another to lift him up. (Eccles. 4:9–10)

We need to steady ourselves on the strong arm of a friend when we stumble. When we're ready to throw in the towel on Christianity because the "abundant life" seems scarce. When the impersonal pink slip appears in our "In" box after thirty years of dedicated service. When we strain to see a light in our dark, dank dungeon of depression.

When we fall, we need a friend. A true friend is there to help us up, not put us down, as Dinah Maria Mulock Craik so vividly illustrates.

> Oh, the comfort—the inexpressible comfort of
>   feeling safe with a person,
> Having neither to weigh thoughts,
> Nor measure words—but pouring them
> All right out—just as they are—
> Chaff and grain together—
> Certain that a faithful hand will
> Take and sift them—
> Keep what is worth keeping—
> And with the breath of kindness
> Blow the rest away.[2]

2. Dinah Maria Mulock Craik, from the *Handbook of Preaching Resources from Literature*, p. 71, as quoted in the study guide *Living Above the Level of Mediocrity* rev. ed., coauthored by Ken Gire, from the Bible-teaching ministry of Charles R. Swindoll (Anaheim, Calif.: Insight for Living, 1994), p. 77.

There's no greater blessing than a friend's encouragement to us when we're weak. But "woe" to those who don't have such a friend (v. 10b). How frightening, how perilous, how lonely to reach out when we've fallen and find no one there.

Who catches you when you fall? Who knows you well enough to sense when you're slipping and loves you enough to pull you up?

Such relationships usually don't crop up overnight. They're cultivated over time. But cultivating deep friendships can be tough plowing, especially for men. Why? Most men were groomed under the macho code: "Real men stand alone. Real men don't cry. Real men don't share their feelings. So suck it up and move on." There's a sophisticated Greek word for that attitude: "Hogwash!"

More men need to open up and admit their frustrations, weaknesses, and fears. That's how friends are made. And relationships are one of the ways God sustains everyone—including men.

A Friend Lends Support When We're Vulnerable

> Furthermore, if two lie down together they keep
> warm, but how can one be warm alone? (v. 11)

When we feel vulnerable and exposed, God often brings His caring touch through the tenderness of a friend. Maybe the cruel hand of divorce has suddenly yanked the security blanket from your life. Maybe your soul still shivers from the doctor's icy prognosis ("It's cancer."). And now your life, your dreams, your family . . . are all a huge question mark. Perhaps you're standing in the unemployment line. Only six years from retirement and you have to start interviewing again. Or what about the news from your teenage daughter that hit like a winter storm ("Mom, Dad, I'm pregnant.").

At times like these, we need the warmth of a friend. Someone who will toss a dry log on the fire and pull his or her soul up close to ours. And wait with us until the night passes.

A Friend Provides Protection When We're Attacked

> And if one can overpower him who is alone, two
> can resist him. (v. 12a)

Lone Ranger Christians make easy targets for Satan's arrows. Don't be fooled. We're never out of Satan's sights. He's always ready to pick off unguarded believers (see 1 Pet. 5:8).

Surprisingly, though, some of the most vicious attacks come from within our own camp, from other believers. Pastors are assailed by critics in the congregation. Power-hungry leaders run over parishioners on their way to the top. Gossips, fresh out of facts but loaded with rumors, wound fellow believers before they can defend themselves.

Whether attacked from within or without, we need the protection of faithful friends. When a member of the congregation poisons our joy with a hateful note, friends remind us that God is using us in the ministry. Friends will set the facts straight when an untruth about us reaches their ears. When everyone else is poised to throw stones, friends will stand between us and the judgmental crowd. And when, in our insecurity, we conjure up an imaginary enemy, friends will help us see the real one, even if it lies within us.

Friends won't lie to protect us or refuse to confront us when we're wrong, but they will stand with us when the assaults come.

Qualities of a True Friend

No one modeled friendship better than our Lord Jesus Christ. His disciples called him Master and Teacher—and He was—but He did more than simply teach His men. He befriended them. He grafted His life into theirs, saw them eye-to-eye, met them at their level. He ministered with them, lived with them. And died for them.

In Jesus' life we see four characteristics of a true friend.

Disregard for Personal Sacrifice

"Greater love has no one than this, that one lay down his life for his friends." (John 15:13)

Most of us have very few friends for whom we would die. But we can probably name several for whom we would gladly sacrifice time, money, or convenience without batting an eye.

The roots of friendship deepen when moistened by the rain of personal sacrifice. True friends give of themselves so others will grow.

Dedication to Mutual Aims

"You are My friends, if you do what I command you." (v. 14)

The best way to demonstrate our commitment to Jesus is to obey His commandments—to show Him that what matters to Him matters to us. Likewise, a sense of oneness in aim and agenda will mark our closest friendships. We'll have a union of philosophy, a shared outlook on life. Do friends ever disagree? Sure they do. But the bedrock values of life will remain undisturbed.

Don't let this scare you away from making friends with nonbelievers, though. Friendship with non-Christians is essential if we're to tell others about the Savior. But you will find that your closest friends have adopted philosophies, goals, and commitments similar to your own.

Discussion of Privileged Information

"No longer do I call you slaves, for the slave does not know what his master is doing; but I have called you friends, for all things that I have heard from My Father I have made known to you." (v. 15)

Jesus has often been portrayed as untouchable, unapproachable —a mysterious man who spoke cryptic messages and couldn't connect with his earthbound followers. How misleading. Jesus opened Himself up, especially to the twelve closest to Him. He shared His heart, His mission, His emotions. He pulled aside the curtain of heaven so His disciples could see the source of His power and wisdom—God the Father.

Friendship goes beyond surface conversation. It shares the deep matters of the heart. Not without discretion. But openly and without fear of ridicule.

Do you have someone to whom you can open up? Someone who's more interested in who you are than how you look or what you wear? Have you given others the freedom to look behind the curtain of your heart? Or do you just want them to see what's on the outside?

Friends get inside. They know things about us that no one else knows. And they're trustworthy enough to repeat only what's appropriate.

Desire to Fulfill Others

"You did not choose Me, but I chose you, and appointed you, that you should go and bear fruit, and that your fruit should remain, that whatever you ask of the Father in My name, He may give to you." (v. 16)

Here's a news flash for believers who picture Jesus as a perpetually dissatisfied taskmaster. He's *for* us. He chose us. He infuses us with life so that we can live for His glory. He's waiting to give to us, if we'll just ask.

Jesus believed in His disciples before they ever believed in themselves. He chose them and trained them for a world-changing mission. That they were simple men didn't bother Him. He saw what they could become. And He invested Himself in their development.

That's what friends do. They invest themselves in the growth, dreams, and success of others. Like a miner's lantern, they expose the glittering veins of potential that run beneath the earthy crust. They help dig, cut, and polish—putting what was once buried on proud display. A friend believes in others and sees the best in them.

So cultivate close friendships. Traveling the spiritual road alone may seem fine for now. But you just might need a friend—or need to be one—at the next intersection.

 Living Insights

You probably know by now that you can't be best friends with everyone. Most of us can count our intimate relationships on one hand. Alan Loy McGinnis, in his insightful book *The Friendship Factor*, emphasizes the importance of balancing quantity with quality in friendships.

> The fact of the matter is that one cannot have a profound connection with more than a few people. Time prohibits it. Deep friendship requires cultivation over the years—evenings before the fire, long walks together, and lots of time for talk. It requires keeping the television off so that the two of you can log in with each other. If your social calendar is too full to provide for such intimate bonding, it should be pared. "True happiness," said Ben Jonson, "consists not in the multitude of friends, but in the worth and choice."
>
> Some people get a strong sense of togetherness from being in large groups of people, and I am not arguing for or against an active social life. What I *am* lobbying for is an ordering of priorities. Getting close to a few people is more important than being popular enough to receive 400 Christmas cards every year.[3]

3. Alan Loy McGinnis, *The Friendship Factor* (Minneapolis, Minn.: Augsburg Publishing House, 1979), p. 24.

Take some time to assess the quality of your friendships. Begin by listing all the people in your life you consider to be friends, even if they're simply acquaintances whose company you enjoy.

_____   _____

_____   _____

_____   _____

_____   _____

_____   _____

Out of that group, list those you call close friends—the ones who share or at least resonate with your life goals and values and know you well enough to ask or give counsel.

_____

_____

_____

_____

Now, who are your intimate friends—those who know you inside and out? You trust them with your secrets and struggles. They're the ones who come at a moment's notice to enter into your joy or sorrow. They have the freedom to confront you, and you're free to do the same with them. Don't be surprised if you only have one or two of these.

_____

_____

If you had trouble coming up with names for the last category, you might need to take some, or one, of your relationships to a deeper level. With whom can you get closer?

_____

How can you start? What about spending more time with that

person or doing more conversation-oriented activities? Find out more about his or her background—and share more about yourself. Write down your thoughts, and start moving toward a richer friendship.

_____

_____

_____

_____

_____

_____

_____

Living Insights

Iron sharpens iron, So one man sharpens another.
(Prov. 27:17)

You may not realize it, but you have a lot to offer. God has given each of us certain abilities, interests, and experiences to use in sharpening others. We were made to gently scrape against the lives of those around us, like a whetting stone against a blade. By being a friend, we can help someone stay sharp in a world that constantly tries to blunt our spiritual edge.

Whom do you sharpen? In whom are you investing? Can you name someone whose metal has potential but requires the patient rasp of a whetting stone? Are you making a difference in someone's life? If so, write down that person's name. Don't be modest.

_____

_____

If you can't come up with a name, give some thought to why others are being deprived of the things you have to offer. Are you too busy? Afraid to get close? Do you lack confidence in yourself or God? What do you think it might be?

_____

_____

_____

16

_____

_____

Now jot down a few of your positive qualities.

_____

_____

_____

_____

See, you do have a lot to offer! Who around you could most benefit from what you have to share?

_____

How can you begin to sharpen that person?

_____

_____

_____

_____

_____

_____

 *Digging Deeper*
_____

How important to God is our involvement with each other? Just take a look at this list of "one anothers" in the New Testament alone. (It will also give you additional ideas on how to be a friend.)

Negative "One-Anothers"

Don't *challenge* one another (Gal. 5:26)
Don't *complain against* one another (James 5:9)
Don't *devour* one another (Gal. 5:15)
Don't *envy* one another (Gal. 5:26)

Don't *judge* one another (Rom. 14:13)
Don't *lie* to one another (Col. 3:9)
Don't *speak against* one another (James 4:11)

Positive "One-Anothers"

Accept one another (Rom. 15:7)
Admonish one another (Rom. 15:14)
Bear one another's burdens (Gal. 6:2)
Bear with one another (Col. 3:13)
Build up one another (1 Thess. 5:11)
Care for one another (1 Cor. 12:25)
Comfort one another (1 Thess. 4:18)
Confess your sins to one another (James 5:16)
Be devoted to one another (Rom. 12:10)
Encourage one another (1 Thess. 5:11)
Fellowship with one another (1 John 1:7)
Forbear with one another (Eph. 4:2)
Forgive one another (Eph. 4:32)
Greet one another (Rom. 16:16)
Honor one another (Rom. 12:10)
Be hospitable to one another (1 Pet. 4:9)
Be humble toward one another (1 Pet. 5:5)
Be kind to one another (Eph. 4:32)
Love one another (John 13:34)
Be at peace with one another (Mark 9:50)
Pray for one another (James 5:16)
Regard one another as more important than oneself (Phil. 2:3)
Be of the *same mind* with one another (Rom. 15:5)
Seek after that which is good for one another (1 Thess. 5:15)
Serve one another (Gal. 5:13)
Stimulate one another to love and good deeds (Heb. 10:24)
Be subject to one another (Eph. 5:21)
Teach one another (Col. 3:16)
Be tenderhearted with one another (Eph. 4:32)
Wait for one another (1 Cor. 11:33)

Chapter 3

DISCOVERING THAT A JOB ISN'T JUST A JOB

Selected Scriptures

I do not like work even when someone else does it.[1]
—Mark Twain

How would you describe your job? A necessary evil? A kind of purgatory to be endured until something better comes along? A ball and chain? Or simply a ball—fun, fulfilling, satisfying?

And where does God fit? Do you think He's relevant to your career? Or does your job seem like a secret room He never enters? Do you see work as one of many facets on life's jewel, interconnected with a larger, brighter purpose? Or is it more like a chunk of granite someone slipped into your backpack—weighing you down as you wander around without direction?

If thinking about your job stirs up feelings of dissatisfaction or discouragement, you're not alone. According to the survey results of researchers James Patterson and Peter Kim, "Only one in ten [Americans] say that they are satisfied with their jobs."[2]

Are you with the other nine? Well, we've got good news: Christians are free to enjoy their careers. God cares deeply about our work—about its quality and character—no matter how minute our tasks may seem. Let's discover His perspective as well as His guidelines for fulfilling ourselves and glorifying Him through our work.

How God Looks at Work

Understanding and appreciating work begins by looking at it through God's eyes. After all, He invented it.

Not a Curse

"How can I expect to get satisfaction from my work; it's part of

---

1. As quoted by Archibald D. Hart in *The Crazy-Making Workplace* (Ann Arbor, Mich.: Servant Publications, Vine Books, 1993), p. 15.

2. James Patterson and Peter Kim, *The Day America Told the Truth* (reprint, New York, N.Y.: Penguin Books, Plume, 1991), p. 155.

the curse." Well-meaning folks, frustrated by unfulfilling employment, often equate work with the curse God gave to Adam (see Gen. 3:17–19). But that's simply not true. God's curse made labor toilsome, but work existed *before* sin's poison seeped into the Garden of Eden. Adam, as the very first human, had this God-given job description:

> Then the Lord God took the man and put him into the garden of Eden to cultivate it and keep it. (2:15)

Landscape management—that was the first job. If you're a farmer, botanist, horticulturist, or someone else who grows and grooms plants, you can be proud. Your career roots (pardon the pun) go all the way back to Adam.

God didn't intend work to be a curse. Although it was affected by the Fall, He originally designed work as part of His perfect creation.

No Sacred/Secular Division

"If I were really spiritual, I would leave my job and become a pastor or missionary." Another comment that reflects a misunderstanding about God's view of work. God doesn't designate one area of life as sacred and another as secular. Whatever work we do, He wants us to reflect His glory and reveal His character.

> Whatever you do, do your work heartily, as for the Lord rather than for men; knowing that from the Lord you will receive the reward of the inheritance. It is the Lord Christ whom you serve. (Col. 3:23–24)

A plumber is no less of a witness for Christ than a preacher. Nor is a mother any less of an evangelist than a missionary. Whether we turn a phrase for a living or turn a wrench, Christ should be the center of our vocation.

Author Doug Sherman reiterates this truth.

> As I have talked to hundreds of workers—in business and the professions, in the military, in government, in education, and in the ministry—I invariably detect a tension between the world of work and the world of religion. . . .
>   . . . I believe that the tension suggests an abnormality: As Christians we have over many years

allowed a chasm to grow between our faith and our day-to-day work, *a chasm that God never intended.*[3] (emphasis added)

Just breeze through the Bible and you'll find that God's greatest champions often honored Him in unspectacular jobs.

- Abraham was a rancher

- Moses and David, shepherds

- Ruth, a grain-gatherer

- Nehemiah, the king's cupbearer

- Jesus, a carpenter

- Peter, a fisherman

- Paul, a tentmaker

God uses real people, not plaster saints—people who sweat and get their hands dirty. As Christians, we're all in the ministry—whether our office is a church building, a skyscraper, or the great outdoors.

That means we need to do our jobs with integrity. Christians should be model employees—employees everyone wants. Unfortunately, that's not always the case.

The Employees Nobody Wants

Now that we know how much God cares about our work, we can focus on how to be godly workers. Let's begin by learning from two employees nobody wants: the sluggard and the deceiver.

The Sluggard

Have you noticed the sluggard in your office? He looks like he's working all day, but actually he's creatively avoiding the real thing. He gets the job done, but only by producing the lowest possible return for a paycheck. Sluggards always do just enough to get by. Lazily eyeing the clock, they live for the end of the day.

As Solomon observed, you can always spot sluggards by the

3. Doug Sherman and William Hendricks, *Your Work Matters to God* (Colorado Springs, Colo.: NavPress, 1987), p. 15.

shoddy work they leave behind.

> I passed by the field of the sluggard,
> And by the vineyard of the man lacking sense;
> And behold, it was completely overgrown with thistles,
> Its surface was covered with nettles,
> And its stone wall was broken down.
> When I saw, I reflected upon it;
> I looked, and received instruction.
> "A little sleep, a little slumber,
> A little folding of the hands to rest,"
> Then your poverty will come as a robber,
> And your want like an armed man.
> (Prov. 24:30–34)

Neglect and procrastination are sluggards' trademarks. They toss work aside to dawdle in leisure. But one day they wake up, look around, and see that their life is a shambles (see also Prov. 6:9–11; 13:4; 15:19; 21:25–26; 26:16).

Don't be a sluggard. Approach your work with vigor and devotion. If your present environment makes that impossible, maybe it's time to change jobs. But first consider that God might have placed you there to make a difference.

The Deceiver

Deceivers dip their hands in the company coffers when nobody's looking. A pen here, a calculator there. A little exaggerating on the time sheet. Calling in sick when there's no illness. Making personal long-distance calls on the company bill. Abandoning principles for profit. Proverbs has something to say about the deceiver too.

> Ill-gotten gains do not profit,
> But righteousness delivers from death. . . .
> The wicked earns deceptive wages,
> But he who sows righteousness gets a true reward.
> (10:2; 11:18)

While stocking up on stolen goods—whether it's paper clips, computer software, or wages—deceivers bankrupt their character. Salary, praise, advancement, bonuses, benefits—all yield lasting dividends only when obtained with integrity.

The Qualities of a Good Employee

Since God calls us to provide for our families through hard work (see 1 Tim. 5:8), and since He also wants our work to honor Him, what qualities, then, should we strive to display as we put bread on the table? Proverbs offers at least three marks of a good employee: diligence, thoughtfulness, and skill.

Diligence

> Poor is he who works with a negligent hand,
> But the hand of the diligent makes rich. (Prov. 10:4)

Notice the parallel construction of the verse. Diligence is the opposite of negligence. Diligent employees pay attention to their work. They stay alert and focused. They take responsibility for a task. They are disciplined, maintaining the same high quality on a project from concept to completion.

A diligent person doesn't have to be poked and prodded into action, since he or she is self-motivated. Diligence encourages a productive and creative work environment, protects us from wasteful distractions, and supplies a needed income as well as inner satisfaction (see also 12:11, 24, 27; 13:4).

Thoughtfulness

Compassion and tact need not suddenly vanish when we show up at the office. Thoughtful employees and employers treat others with respect, recognizing their value and contribution to the company. Proverbs even urges those in an agricultural society to appreciate their animals.

> A righteous man has regard for the life of his beast,
> But the compassion of the wicked is cruel.
> (Prov. 12:10)

How much more, then, should we appreciate those with whom we work (see also 27:17)?

Now a word especially for you bosses.

> Like a roaring lion and a rushing bear
> Is a wicked ruler over a poor people.
> A leader who is a great oppressor lacks understanding,
> But he who hates unjust gain will prolong his
> days. . . .

Know well the condition of your flocks,
And pay attention to your herds. (28:15–16; 27:23)

Do you want to be a good boss? Do you want to have the respect of your subordinates? Then treat them like people, not numbers. Be genuinely concerned about your employees' lives. Remember, God's purpose for them includes their job but goes beyond it too. And strive to understand their unique skills and ways of working.

Thoughtfulness can take you beyond wise leadership; it can transform you into a person who makes a positive, lasting impact on another's life.

Skill

Do you see a man skilled in his work?
He will stand before kings;
He will not stand before obscure men.
(Prov. 22:29)

Are you skilled at what you do? Do you perform your job with expertise and resourcefulness? Are you committed to growing, to constantly developing and widening the range of your abilities? Companies and ministries need people with a knack for detail and a passion for excellence.

Remember, your job is not just a job. It's a calling, a ministry, a God-ordained activity. It's bigger than nine to five. It's part of eternity.

 Living Insights STUDY ONE

Let's go back to our opening question. How would you describe your job? If you love what you do, if your work brings fulfillment and satisfaction, if you're convinced God has placed you in exactly the right place, you can skip these Living Insights. If, however, your position causes more frustration than satisfaction, if you feel stuck in a dead-end job, let's delve a little deeper into how to make the most of your work.

Read through the following five common causes of job dissatisfaction (we'll cover three in this study and the rest in Study Two). Write down anything about your situation that needs attention. Be as specific as you can.

Unbiblical Work Habits

Lazy and dishonest employees are usually dissatisfied employees. Such character flaws keep us from doing our best. And the burden of guilt can slow us down.

Maybe the answer to your job satisfaction problem involves blending some of the principles from this chapter into your work habits. Do you need to get to the office earlier? Or leave a little later? Or simply work harder and smarter while you're there? Are you compromising your integrity in any way? How are you treating your coworkers? Maybe building stronger relationships with them will make your job more palatable.

_____

_____

_____

_____

_____

Unrealistic Expectations

Though work itself is not a curse, it has been tainted (as has all of creation) by sin. Our jobs are harder, more taxing than they would be in a perfect world. So work exhausts us and often steers us into conflict with others. Sin makes bosses and subordinates harder to deal with—it makes *us* harder to deal with. In the workplace, sin's invisible fingers never stop tugging at the garment of our faith.

Yes, our work matters to God. He does care about our satisfaction. He does see our occupation as meaningful. He does want to shine His light through our labor. However, we must balance those truths with another: In a sin-infected world, there is no perfect job, even in ministry. If we expect our careers to protect us from all insecurity and adversity or to meet our deepest spiritual needs, we have unrealistic expectations which lead to dissatisfaction.

_____

_____

_____

Unhealthy Attachment to Money

Though Scripture doesn't condemn money, it does warn against the improper use of it. For Christians, the rule of thumb is this: Don't pursue money as an end in itself, an idol to be set up and worshiped. Rather, use it as a tool for God's glory. Whether we acquire little or much, we need to keep our possessions in proper perspective (see Matt. 6:24–34; 1 Tim. 6:17–19).

When material gain climbs to the top of the priority list, when contentment becomes covetousness, we've lost God's perspective on money. There's not a thing wrong with expecting a fair wage for our labor. But if all we want out of a job is money, we'll never be satisfied. We'll always want more, filling our eyes so full of dollar signs that we lose sight of God's plan for our lives.

 Living Insights STUDY TWO

Let's continue assessing your job by looking at two more causes of job dissatisfaction.

Unfamiliarity with Our Own Abilities

Authors Arthur Miller and Ralph Mattson contend that we cannot find real satisfaction in employment without first discovering our unique, God-given design.

> The world, for the most part, assumes you are something to be molded or manipulated or shaped or trained or taught—that you are the raw material for someone else's intentions. Our contention is that

you have a design of your own—God's blueprint—
and can only be fulfilled when you carry out that
design, regardless of how high or low on the ladder
of success you are.[4]

The Scriptures concur that we're not random creations. God
crafted our intricate bodies and souls and gave us spiritual gifts at
salvation (see Ps. 139; Rom. 12:4–8; 1 Cor. 12).

So if you feel stuck in the wrong job, you just might be. There's
a reason we're not all performing the same tasks. We're different!
Someone who freezes up in front of an audience probably shouldn't
pursue preaching as a career. Those who can't discern one note
from another won't make very good musicians. A disdain for numbers doesn't mix with the accounting profession. Can't stand animals? Don't go to veterinary school. You get the picture.

All this doesn't mean that God can't help us grow and improve
or overcome fears. He can and does. It does mean, however, that
dissatisfaction can result from our trying to hammer ourselves into
a career hole that's clearly a mismatch for our design.

What are you good at? What do you love to do? What tasks,
what kinds of people and situations give you the most satisfaction?
Toward what kinds of projects have you gravitated in the past,
regardless of your "official" job descriptions? These are the kinds of
questions to ask in order to determine your divine design.[5]

_____

_____

_____

_____

_____

Unhealthy Work Environment

You wondered if we would get here, didn't you? Yes, it's possible
that you're just in an unhealthy situation. Some bosses seem to enjoy

4. Arthur F. Miller and Ralph T. Mattson, *The Truth about You: Discover What You Should
Be Doing with Your Life* (Old Tappan, N.J.: Fleming H. Revell Co., 1977), p. 15.

5. If you want to explore this topic further, we recommend Miller and Mattson's book *The
Truth about You.*

abusing subordinates. Some are unfair, jealous, insecure, paranoid. They bring a briefcase full of problems to work every day and unload it on their employees. Perhaps you've had enough.

Has overtime become the norm instead of the exception? Maybe you're tired of the pressure to compromise your integrity. Have you simply outgrown the position or the company? Maybe neither fits your own plans and goals any longer.

We all have limits. You have to determine yours. After praying, talking with your family and friends, and considering all the options, if you feel it's time to go—go. And don't look back. God most likely has something better.

The next step is up to you. You may need to change your work habits. Or alter your expectations. Or inventory your abilities. Or confront your boss. Or change jobs. Or focus on something besides money. Write down whatever steps you need to take.

_____

_____

_____

_____

_____

_____

_____

_____

_____

_____

Chapter 4

DISCOVERING THE MISSING JEWEL OF WORSHIP

Isaiah 6:1–8

W hatever happened to worship? A. W. Tozer observed that worship

> is the missing jewel in modern evangelicalism. We're organized; we work; we have our agendas. We have almost everything, but there's one thing that the churches, even the gospel churches, do not have: that is the ability to worship. We are not cultivating the art of worship. It's the one shining gem that is lost to the modern church, and I believe that we ought to search for this until we find it.[1]

A ring that has lost its diamond. Structure without beauty. Mere activity instead of awe. Such is the state of much of modern Christianity. In another writer's words, we've substituted "playing church" for worshiping God.[2]

"Amen, brother!" when the sermon's good. Jump up and clap hands—look the part of impassioned praise. Or stand up, sit down, kneel now, and pray. Eyes closed, head bowed, look somber and contrite. Here comes the offering plate—dutifully drop in a dollar. Last song. Shake the pastor's hand. "Wanna go out for lunch? Where did I put the keys?"

Where did we put God?

It's amazing how we can be in God's house all morning and sometimes never see Him, never worship, in the midst of our routine.

Are you longing for something deeper? Do you sense that there's something more precious to be found? Then grab your flashlight and let's find this dazzling gem, study it, and see how we can restore it to its proper place.

---

1. A. W. Tozer, "Worship: The Normal Employment of Moral Beings," in *The Best of A. W. Tozer*, comp. Warren W. Wiersbe (Grand Rapids Mich.: Baker Book House, 1978; reprint, Camp Hill, Pa.: Christian Publications, 1991), pp. 217–18.

2. Anne Ortlund, *Up with Worship: How to Quit Playing Church*, rev. ed. (Ventura, Calif.: Gospel Light Publications, Regal Books, 1982), p. 10.

Worship Illuminated

Ronald Allen and Gordon Borror, in their book *Worship: Rediscovering the Missing Jewel*, shine a light on what worship really is.

> *Worship is an active response to God whereby we declare His worth.* Worship is not passive, but is participative. Worship is not simply a mood; it is a response. Worship is not just a feeling; it is a declaration. . . .
> The English word worship is wonderfully expressive of the act that it describes. This term comes from the Anglo-Saxon *weorthscipe*, which then was modified to *worthship*, and finally to *worship*. Worship means "to attribute worth" to something or someone.[3]

Ascribing to God His supreme worth—that's the dazzling gem that has been snatched from its setting. We focus on the sermon's worth, the preacher's worth, the music's worth, the missionaries' worth—even the nursery's worth! And these are all wonderful. But too often we stop there and don't allow them to take us beyond themselves to God. Worship, in the church, includes each part of the service but takes us further. Worship is transcendent, bringing us into the presence and glory of God.

How can we restore this priceless gem, this declaration of God's immeasurable worth, to our churches today? Let's learn from the prophet Isaiah, whose experience of worship forever changed his life.

Isaiah's Worship Experience

Any jewel sparkles brighter against a dark backdrop, and the jewel of worship is no exception. In Isaiah's day, the backdrop was Judah, a nation empowered by military might and financial security that had grown self-sufficient and indifferent toward God. Presumption had replaced gratitude. Pride had usurped reverence. Judah's king, Uzziah, personified this attitude when he brazenly entered the temple to burn incense—a duty reserved solely for priests. God struck the proud king with leprosy, and Uzziah lived out the rest of his life in shameful quarantine (see 2 Chron. 26). His godly son took the throne upon Uzziah's death, but the nation "continued acting corruptly" (27:2).

3. Ronald Allen and Gordon Borror, *Worship: Rediscovering the Missing Jewel* (Portland, Oreg.: Multnomah Press, 1982), p. 16.

Enter Isaiah, the prophet who would restore the luster of worship to Judah. But God first had to make him a worshiper. Let's examine Isaiah's encounter with God under the jeweler's loupe so that we can reclaim the missing gem of worship for our own church experience.

He Saw the Lord

> In the year of King Uzziah's death, I saw the Lord sitting on a throne, lofty and exalted, with the train of His robe filling the temple. Seraphim stood above Him, each having six wings; with two he covered his face, and with two he covered his feet, and with two he flew. (Isa. 6:1–2)

How significant that in the midst of a people who had lost sight of God, Isaiah's vision would open with his seeing the living Lord on His throne. God was "lofty and exalted," His glory filling the temple. And so holy was His presence that even the seraphim[4] had to shield their eyes as they sang praises around His throne.

> And one called out to another and said,
> "Holy, Holy, Holy, is the Lord of hosts,
> The whole earth is full of His glory."
> And the foundations of the thresholds trembled at the voice of him who called out, while the temple was filling with smoke. (vv. 3–4)

This celestial worship service literally rocked the foundations of the temple! In their antiphony of praise, the angels thundered, "Holy, Holy, Holy." This repetition doesn't reflect a lack of lyrical creativity; rather, whenever a word is used three times in a row in Scripture, it signifies the infinite. The Lord of hosts, they sing, is infinitely holy.

So here's where worship begins—with our eyes fixed on the holy Lord of heaven. When we come for worship on Sunday morning, we should be looking for God. Our hearts should be attuned to His heart, our souls open to drink in His glory.

---

4. Seraphim (plural for *seraph*) are angelic creatures mentioned only here in Isaiah 6:2, 6. The Hebrew root means "burn." "These angelic beings were brilliant as flaming fire, symbolic of the purity and power of the heavenly court." *Theological Wordbook of the Old Testament*, ed. R. Laird Harris, Gleason L. Archer, Jr., Bruce K. Waltke (Chicago, Ill.: Moody Press, 1980), vol. 2, p. 884.

All too often, though, we're surrounded by distractions that would drag us down from the heavenlies—even in church. Memories of the breakfast spat with our spouse or plans for this week's big presentation at the office swirl around in our minds. Not to mention the people who fill the pews—Mr. Johnson with his bad breath and out-of-style sport coat, the Mitchell twins making confetti out of the church bulletin, and that lady behind us with the honking cold.

If we think Satan doesn't accompany us to church, we're mistaken. He'll do everything he can to distract us from worshiping God. So we must come with our spiritual eyes open, looking for the Lord in the message, the music, and the fellowship.

He Was Touched by the Lord

> Then I said,
> "Woe is me, for I am ruined!
> Because I am a man of unclean lips,
> And I live among a people of unclean lips;
> For my eyes have seen the King, the Lord of
> hosts." (v. 5)

In the burning light of the Lord's holiness, Isaiah saw in desperation his own dark sin and corruption. "I am ruined," he cried out, "I am a man of unclean lips, living among a people of unclean lips!" In other words, a sinner living among sinners.[5] How else can one respond when confronted with God's holiness? We may think we're living a pretty good life until our flaws show up under the radiance of His revealing light.

The Lord, however, didn't abandon Isaiah in his sinfulness.

> Then one of the seraphim flew to me, with a burning coal in his hand which he had taken from the altar with tongs. And he touched my mouth with it and said, "Behold, this has touched your lips; and your iniquity is taken away, and your sin is forgiven." (vv. 6–7)

5. Isaiah, though greatly used by God, still had a sinful nature, as did the people to whom he ministered. Commentators generally agree that the prophet's admission of "unclean lips" signifies his awareness of his sinful nature in light of God's holiness. "Unclean lips," however, might also indicate that Isaiah struggled with a particular sin of the tongue, such as profanity, which he needed to confess to receive God's cleansing.

God touched Isaiah with the cleansing fire of forgiveness. This shows that worship isn't something to be checked off our religious "to do" list; it's an experience God uses to meet us at our point of need. After beholding God's glory, Isaiah saw his own sinfulness more clearly than ever. He, like all of us, needed hope that a sinful human could stand before a holy God without fear of judgment.

Notice that the angel with the burning coal flew *to Isaiah* (v. 6). God knew the prophet's need and set the solution in motion. The Holy reached out to the hopeless. The Light delved into the darkness. What a picture of the forgiveness God provides for us in Christ.

> In the presence of the Lord, we are all unclean and even the fiery seraphim are not clean before Him or worthy to behold Him. How fortunate, however, that Christ as the Priestly King has not only an exalted *throne*, but also an *altar*, where sins can be burned away, as happened with this seer.[6]

Because of Jesus Christ, we can approach God without being consumed by His holiness. Just as God sent the seraph to cleanse Isaiah's lips, He sent Christ to cleanse our hearts and open the door to God's throne room.

Remember, then, that when our own sinfulness overwhelms us, God places a burning coal of forgiveness on our hearts with His Word. When the mess we've made of life seems too big even for God to clean up, He encourages us with a hymn of His sufficiency and power. When Christianity seems like a mundane list of religious obligations, He meets us at His table, where the bread and wine remind us that our faith rests in a Person—One who gave His life for us.

Our needs are great. God's resources are infinite. In worship, He touches our deepest needs.

He Heard from the Lord

> Then I heard the voice of the Lord, saying, "Whom shall I send, and who will go for Us?" (v. 8a)

From the angels' "Holy, Holy, Holy" and the seraph's "Your sin is forgiven," Isaiah next heard the very voice of the Lord. "Who will go for Us?" asked the Triune God. Though Isaiah had felt sinful

---

6. Harry Bultema, *Commentary on Isaiah,* trans. Cornelius Lambregtse (Muskegon, Mich.: Bereer Publishing, 1923, Grand Rapids, Mich.: Kregel Publications, 1981), p. 96.

and worthless, he received not only forgiveness but an offer to serve. How gracious of God to come close to Isaiah and affirm his value and usefulness.

Worship, for us, also reinforces our sense of purpose. We praise God, confess our sins, and evaluate our lives as He speaks to our hearts. So we must *listen*. We never know which part of the worship service God might use to enlighten us, convict us, or stir us to action.

He Responded to the Lord

Then I said, "Here am I. Send me!" (v. 8b)

Eager and grateful to his awesome yet tender God, Isaiah shouted, "Me! I'll go for You. Please send me!" So God honored his willing heart. And it was through Isaiah's lips that the people heard:

"A virgin will be with child."

"The people who walk in darkness
Will see a great light."

"Those who wait for the Lord . . . will mount up with wings like eagles."

"All of us like sheep have gone astray."

"'My thoughts are not your thoughts,
Neither are your ways My ways.'"

"We are the clay, and Thou our potter."[7]

Worship, as Isaiah shows us, doesn't end with simply listening to God. It also calls for a response on our part. And who knows, God just may use us to be an Isaiah for our age—bringing good news to the afflicted, binding up the brokenhearted, proclaiming freedom to captives, comforting those who mourn (see 61:1–2). When we worship, let us do so with willing and responsive hearts.

Four Principles for Worship

Do you see how this jewel glimmers? Surely, we don't ever want to lose it again. These four principles will help us hold on to it more tightly.

---

7. See Isaiah 7:14; 9:2; 40:31; 53:6; 55:8; 64:8.

1. *A deep sense of need draws us to worship.* God designed worship for people who need Him. Isaiah needed to see the grandeur of God's holiness and majesty. He needed to know the depth of his own sin and dependency. And he needed to experience the relief of the Lord's forgiveness. God met Isaiah's needs, and He meets ours.

2. *Preoccupation with the Lord enhances worship.* The Lord is the object of our worship. So let's preoccupy ourselves with *Him.* Not the pastor. Not the music. Not the facilities. Not the programs. These are merely means to the end of worshiping God. If your worship is drawn to something or someone other than the Lord, try spending some time focusing on Him before the next service—perhaps on Saturday night or early Sunday morning. Read the Scriptures, sing, pray, reflect. Then enter the sanctuary with one goal in mind—to meet God.

3. *Worship is a corporate effort.* Since each believer is part of the local assembly, what we do as individuals affects the corporate worship experience. Even if you can't carry a tune in a bucket, you still contribute to the worship. The heartfelt voices of His united people ring out as beautifully as the flaming praises of the seraphim.

4. *Worship depends on honesty, humility, and availability.* "I don't have it all together; I need to hear from God." "Lord, You're the master; I'm the servant. What would You have me do?" "Wherever You send me, I'll go." Confessions like these reveal the underlying attitudes of worship. Worship is a time to open up, not cover up. God knows our needs anyway, so why try to hide them? Worship simply can't shimmer in the fog of deceit, pride, and inflexibility. Open up, and let Him shine.

See how much better the ring looks with the stone of worship in place? It's hard to take your eyes off of it, isn't it? Treasure it, enjoy it. And whatever you do, don't lose it.

 Living Insights

We never know what God will use to stir our souls to worship. I'll never forget the Sunday He used a nine-year-old violinist. Her performance was more than a song. It was a sermon.

———◆———

Her name was Emily. As the offering plates circulated around the sanctuary, she began to play. Her skill was stunning. I glanced around the auditorium and noticed the crowd was fixed on her every movement. Some leaned forward, so their ears would not have to wait a second longer than necessary to receive the next note. As she coaxed hauntingly beautiful sounds from her instrument, my eyes filled with tears.

Emily's music was the only detectable sound. There was no fidgeting in the congregation, no coughing. Only the captivated faces of men and women who watched and wondered at this elegant display of God's grace, this prodigy in a ruffled dress and hair band. A standing ovation erupted the instant she finished.

The next day I tried to figure out why Emily's presentation touched us so. I think it's because we're caught off guard when God shines His glory through such an unlikely agent. We *expect* God to use the sermon and the singing. We *expect* eloquence and precision from the preacher and the choir or worship team. Some of us even attend churches that use state-of-the-art audiovisual equipment to aid in worship.

But along comes little Emily. No theology degree. No oratory skill. In fact, not a word at all. Just a humble instrument and pretty smile. Who would have expected her to be the one to lead us to the Father's throne room? We would have been pleased for her to simply try. But she wowed us! With her first note, she changed from a little girl to a kind of receiver, tuned to an angelic frequency. And for a moment, we heard the strings of heaven.

It seems that God delights in surprising us, in bursting through our walls of religious predictability. I, for one, am glad. The spiritual life can become routine if we let it. It sometimes feels as dutiful and compartmentalized as the slots in our weekly calendar, as if God has lost His spontaneity. In the monotony of mechanical spirituality, we forget that He is a Person. And we feel dry as dust.

But I know of one Sunday when the worship service lived up to its name. If cobwebs dangled from any hearts that morning, God swept them away with the rosined bow of a nine-year-old girl.

Thank you, Emily, for reminding us that some of the best sermons come from the most unlikely messengers. And that God has given us all gifts that will honor Him—if we will only use them. Play on, little sister. Play on.[8]

8. Gary Matlack, adapted from "Emily's Sermon" © 1993.

Living Insights

Worship, like anything, can swing to extremes. On one end of the spectrum is unbridled emotionalism, where you feel out of place if you're not sweating or being "slain in the Spirit." On the other end are the holy embalmed, those who stiffly file into the service each week to choke down another dusty dose of doctrine. Neither extreme is biblical, as author John Piper explains.

> Jesus says, "The hour is coming, and now is, when the true worshipers will worship the Father in spirit and truth." . . .
>
> Worshiping in spirit is the opposite of worshiping in merely external ways. It is the opposite of empty formalism and traditionalism. Worshiping in truth is the opposite of worship based on an inadequate view of God. Worship must have heart and head. Worship must engage emotions and thought.
>
> Truth without emotion produces dead orthodoxy and a church full (or half-full) of artificial admirers (like people who write generic anniversary cards for a living). On the other hand, emotion without truth produces empty frenzy and cultivates shallow people who refuse the discipline of rigorous thought. But true worship comes from people who are deeply emotional and who love deep and sound doctrine. Strong affections for God rooted in truth are the bone and marrow of biblical worship.[9]

Where do you fall on the worship scale? Isaiah managed to find the right balance between knowing his needs and listening to God's voice. As you contemplate Isaiah's example and Piper's words, what is needed in your worship?

_____

_____

_____

9. John Piper, *Desiring God: Meditations of a Christian Hedonist* (Portland, Oreg.: Multnomah Press, 1986), p. 65.

Chapter 5

DISCOVERING THE DIFFERENCE BETWEEN GOD'S WAYS AND OUR WAYS

Genesis 45:1–8; 50:18–21; Romans 8:28–32

Rick pulled the plane ticket from the inside pocket of his blazer and smiled. After sitting through two days of lectures on invasive cardiology procedures at the New Orleans Hilton, the doctor longed to see the Dallas skyline. He always liked coming home. But especially today—his tenth wedding anniversary.

Tonight, after dropping off the kids with Jill's parents, the two of them would enjoy an elegant dinner at the French Room, then stay overnight at the Adolphus—where they'd spent their honeymoon. But things don't always turn out as planned . . .

On the other end of the phone, Jill was crying. "But everything's set, Rick," she said. "I've been looking forward to this for so long."

"I know, honey; so have I," Rick responded. "I'm so sorry. I got bumped from the flight—some stupid computer glitch. They'll put me up in a hotel, and I'll be home tomorrow around noon. We'll still have our celebration. It'll just be a little delayed."

The conversation ended with two sincere but disappointed "I love yous."

Feeling helpless and mishandled, Rick took the matter up with God. "Lord, I know You could have prevented this. In fact, I believe You could still get me back on that flight if You wanted to. How could You leave me stranded here?"

Later that night, while watching the ten o'clock news in his hotel room, Rick saw images of what was left of the plane from which he had been bumped. It had crashed in the Gulf of Mexico. There were no survivors.

He reached for the phone, trembling, and called home. He and Jill would never forget this anniversary.

◆

Our sovereign Lord operates from an eternal agenda, not a daily planner. Sometimes, when we expect Him to charge over the hill with the cavalry, He holds back. Other times, at the exact moment we think He has misplaced our address, He comes in through the back door. And when we wonder if we'll ever again feel His warmth, He pulls us in from the cold and sets us in front of His crackling fire.

Is God approachable? Yes. Aware of our most intimate needs? Absolutely. Caring? Always. Yet He is beyond figuring out. Not because He delights in some sort of cosmic cat-and-mouse game, but because He's God. Even with all He has revealed about Himself in His Word, His hand often moves in ways we can't explain.

Do you need a reminder that the Creator is still involved with His creation? That the Potter still sits at His wheel? Then let's explore His trustworthy sovereignty, first in Joseph's life and then in God's promise to us in Romans 8.

God at Work in Joseph's Life

God took Joseph from a literal pit to the pinnacle of power in Egypt. His story reminds us that God's hand is never idle, even when we feel as if we've slipped through His fingers.

From Pit to Pinnacle

Joseph began life as his father's favorite. This, coupled with his divine dreams that his whole family would someday bow before him, enflamed the hatred of his brothers. One day, seething with contempt and rage, they plotted to murder him, but the eldest brother persuaded the others merely to throw Joseph into a pit. Then, without the knowledge of the eldest brother, they sold him as a slave to a caravan of Ishmaelites bound for Egypt. Joseph's multicolored tunic, drenched in goat's blood by his scheming siblings, convinced their father that he had been killed by a wild beast (Gen. 37). But he was very much alive.

In Egypt, God blessed Joseph with success as Potiphar's servant and, eventually, as the overseer of all his possessions. Potiphar's wife, however, tried to seduce Joseph. When he resisted and ran, she angrily claimed that he had tried to rape her. So Potiphar threw his once-trusted employee in prison (39:1–20).

God, though, was with Joseph in prison. Joseph gained the trust and respect of the chief jailer, who put him in charge of the prisoners. The Lord also gave Joseph the ability to interpret dreams, which he did for two of his cell mates—officials in Pharaoh's court. One of the men promised to put in a good word for Joseph upon his release, but he forgot. And Joseph remained in jail for two more years (39:21–41:1a).

When Pharaoh had a troubling dream, however, that forgetful official finally remembered Joseph, and he was summoned from the dungeon. God not only gave Joseph the interpretation of the dream—which warned of approaching famine—He also provided Joseph a plan for survival. Impressed by Joseph's wisdom and discernment, Pharaoh bestowed on him the second highest position in the land. Among other duties, Joseph supervised the storage and distribution of Egypt's grain during the famine (chap. 41). And guess who came to buy food?

The Moment of Truth

Joseph's brothers had no idea that the man before whom they bowed—the second most powerful man in all of Egypt—was the brother they had plucked from their lives and flicked aside like a bothersome thorn. The moment finally came, though, for Joseph to reveal his true identity.

> Then Joseph could not control himself before all those who stood by him, and he cried, "Have everyone go out from me." So there was no man with him when Joseph made himself known to his brothers. And he wept so loudly that the Egyptians heard it, and the household of Pharaoh heard of it. Then Joseph said to his brothers, "I am Joseph! Is my father still alive?" (Gen. 45:1–3a)

Imagine his brothers' emotions—shock, guilt, fear. Joseph's revelation struck them speechless.

> But his brothers could not answer him, for they were dismayed at his presence. Then Joseph said to his brothers, "Please come closer to me." And they came closer. And he said, "I am your brother Joseph, whom you sold into Egypt." (vv. 3b–4)

What would you have done in Joseph's place? He had the authority to order the instant death of his brothers. And no one, including Pharaoh, would have questioned his decision. But rather than raising his own hand in judgment, Joseph recognized God's hand in preserving his family.

"And now do not be grieved or angry with yourselves, because you sold me here; for God sent me before you to preserve life. For the famine has been in the land these two years, and there are still five years in which there will be neither plowing nor harvesting. And God sent me before you to preserve for you a remnant in the earth, and to keep you alive by a great deliverance. Now, therefore, it was not you who sent me here, but God; and He has made me a father to Pharaoh and lord of all his household and ruler over all the land of Egypt." (vv. 5–8)

What perspective! "God was in it from the beginning." It took fifteen years, but now Joseph was finally reunited with his family, finally able to embrace his beloved father again.

Later, when their father died, all the old guilt and fears stormed the brothers' hearts, and they cringed in anticipation of Joseph's rightful vengeance. Yet Joseph's attitude remained the same.

Then his brothers also came and fell down before him and said, "Behold, we are your servants." But Joseph said to them, "Do not be afraid, for am I in God's place? And as for you, you meant evil against me, but God meant it for good in order to bring about this present result, to preserve many people alive." (50:18–20)

"Am I in God's place?" Joseph asked. Interesting, isn't it? The more we acknowledge God's sovereignty, the less we assail others or hold grudges against them for our difficulties. Recognizing God's sovereignty even allows us to forgive.

"So therefore, do not be afraid; I will provide for you and your little ones." So he comforted them and spoke kindly to them. (v. 21)

Coming to grips with God's sovereignty doesn't mean we deny reality—Joseph plainly told his brothers that they "meant evil against" him. God's sovereignty doesn't guarantee pain-free living either. But acknowledging it will help us see more of life, including pain, as under God's absolute control.

Even when our lives seem to get hung up in neutral, God's agenda cruises along. It simply cannot be sidetracked. Joseph's brothers couldn't sabotage Joseph's destiny. Instead, they unwittingly participated in God's eternal plan for salvation. Making their brother a slave resulted in their release from the bondage of famine. And from this small family grew the Hebrew nation, from which the Messiah would come—to release us all from the bondage of sin.

God at Work in Our Lives

Let's move from the courts of Pharaoh to the streets of Rome. Believers in that city, living under the constant shadow of persecution, needed a reminder that God still stirred on behalf of His people. So the apostle Paul took up his pen of encouragement and wrote,

> And we know that God causes all things to work together for good to those who love God, to those who are called according to His purpose. (Rom. 8:28)

How often we reach into the medicine cabinet of Scripture for that verse, hoping to ease the sting of divorce, job loss, or the untimely death of a child. Paul's words, though, are more than a salve to be spread lightly over a wound. They're food for our souls, meant to strengthen our faith in the sovereign Lord of the universe, who wants us to see our lives as part of His plan. Let's stop and savor four key topics that emerge from Paul's words to the Romans: God's promise, providence, project, and provision.

God's Promise

Romans 8:28 is a promise. Not a "name it, claim it" formula for instant blessing, but a statement to Christians about God—a truth on which we can depend. "We know," says the apostle. Not "we think" or "we're fairly certain." This is an accepted truth for believers to fall back on.

The promise emerges from something deeper than Paul's desire to encourage the Romans. It's rooted in God Himself. "We know that *God causes.*" He's the reason we can hang on to this verse with assurance. Our infinite, infallible Lord is in complete control.

How do we know God's in control? Because the verse assures us that He's working for the accomplishment of *His* purpose— which often differs from what *we* had in mind. In life's vast orchestra, we may not always recognize the music or know why one song is chosen over another, but God knows. And He somehow puts "all things" together in a concert that brings glory to Himself.

God's Providence

The word *providence* is often used as a synonym for God's control of the universe. In its simplest form, it means "to foresee." But it involves much more, as the Westminster Confession of Faith expresses:

> God, the great Creator of all things, doth uphold, direct, dispose, and govern all creatures, actions, and things, from the greatest even to the least, by his most wise and holy providence, according to his infallible foreknowledge and the free and immutable counsel of his own will, to the praise of the glory of his wisdom, power, justice, goodness, and mercy.[1]

What God creates, He also sustains. Nowhere is that more necessary than in the salvation of His people, which Paul addresses in Romans 8:29–30.

> For whom He foreknew, He also predestined to become conformed to the image of His Son, that He might be the first-born among many brethren; and whom He predestined, these He also called; and whom He called, these He also justified; and whom He justified, these He also glorified.

How encouraging! God chose us long before we were interested in Him. He forgave us, and delivered us from the eternal penalty of sin. But He didn't stop there.

God's Project

God is still at work, transforming us into Christ's likeness until He takes us home.

> He also predestined [us] to become conformed to the image of His Son. (v. 29b)

Aren't you glad that your spiritual growth doesn't depend solely on you? What if the development of such Christlike qualities as patience, gentleness, forgiveness, love, and humility depended on our own natural ability? Without Christ's example? Without the Holy Spirit's indwelling presence? Impossible.

---

1. John H. Leith, ed., *Creeds of the Churches*, 3d ed. (Louisville, Ky.: John Knox Press, 1982), p. 200.

Maybe you've seen the bumper sticker "Be patient; God isn't finished with me yet." Trite, yes. But true, according to Paul. We're like an incomplete painting propped against God's easel. A whisk of the brush here, a daub of color there. A little mixing. A little shading. The longer He works, the more like Christ we look. You might say we're a masterpiece in the making.

God's Provision

There's more good news.

> What then shall we say to these things? If God is for us, who is against us? He who did not spare His own Son, but delivered Him up for us all, how will He not also with Him freely give us all things? (vv. 31–32)

God is so much *for* us that He gave us Christ, His own Son, crucified. And, explains commentator Everett F. Harrison,

> with the cross before us as the mighty demonstration of God's grace in giving his dearest to help the neediest, it naturally follows that the same gracious spirit will not withhold anything from those who are his.[2] (See also 2 Pet. 1:3.)

That's His provision. We need to stash it away and pull it out when we think He's plotting against us. Or when stress and interpersonal conflicts threaten to unravel us. When we think He has disowned us, forgotten us. When walking with Him seems more like stacking random concrete blocks than building a beautiful cathedral. We need to remember that we stopped being God's enemy when we trusted Christ. Jesus has reconciled us to God (see Rom. 5:10–11).

Yes, God still allows the rain of adversity to fall on His children. But like a loving father, He also has hold of the umbrella.

His ways are not our ways. But His ways are always right.

2. Everett F. Harrison, "Romans," in *The Expositor's Bible Commentary*, ed. Frank E. Gaebelein (Grand Rapids, Mich.: Zondervan Publishing House, Regency Reference Library, 1976), vol. 10, pp. 98–99.

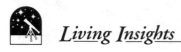

Have you ever considered the differences between the theistic and deistic views of God?

> Theism is the belief that there is a God both *beyond* and *within* the world, a Creator and Sustainer who sovereignly controls the world and supernaturally intervenes in it. Deism holds with theism that God created the world but denies his supernatural intervention in it on the grounds that the world operates by natural and self-sustaining laws of the Creator. In short, God is *beyond* the world but he is not active in the world in a supernatural way.[3]

Which of these views did Joseph and Paul embrace?

_____

How can you tell?

_____

_____

_____

_____

If Joseph were a deist, would he have said, "Do not be afraid, for am I in God's place? And as for you, you meant evil against me, but God meant it for good in order to bring about this present result, to preserve many people alive" (Gen. 50:19–20)? How do you think he would have responded to his brothers?

_____

_____

_____

_____

3. Norman L. Geisler, *Christian Apologetics* (Grand Rapids, Mich.: Baker Book House, 1976), p. 151.

How would the promise of Romans 8:28 read if Paul had been a deist?

_____

_____

_____

_____

How can we blend more of our theistic beliefs into daily living? In other words, how can we live as though we really believe God is in control? Let the following verses get your thoughts started.

Philippians 4:6–7 _____

_____

Matthew 7:7–11 _____

_____

Psalm 119:89–96 _____

_____

Living Insights

God is sovereign. Infinitely powerful and holy. So He can even turn sin around to accomplish His purposes. The evil act of Joseph's brothers landed Joseph in Egypt, where he was able to preserve the Hebrew remnant (see Gen. 50:18–20). With God's permission, Satan unleashed his fury on Job, who came to embrace God's sovereignty through suffering (see Job 42:1–6).

The most vivid example, though, is the crucifixion of Jesus Christ. The Lord was betrayed by Judas and put to death by the hands of evil men. Yet God used their sinful act to provide a way of salvation for sinners just like them (see Acts 2:22–24).

What does God's sovereignty over sin tell you about His ability to turn bad things into good?

_____

_____

_____

_____

_____

Does God's authority over everything, including sin, tell you anything about how He might be working in an area of your life that's out of your control? What hope does that give you?

_____

_____

_____

_____

Chapter 6

DISCOVERING YOUR PART IN REACHING THE LOST

Acts 8:25–40

Since Disneyland opened on July 17, 1955, more than 300 million guests have clicked through the turnstiles—and they're still coming. Why?

They come to brave bubbling pools of lava and poison darts on the Indiana Jones Adventure ride. They can't wait to dodge the cannon fire of the raucous buccaneers in Pirates of the Caribbean, crest the white peaks of the Matterhorn, and plummet through the dark cosmos of Space Mountain. And who could pass up that dizzy, green feeling from the teacup ride? They line Main Street to watch the spectacular parades such as the Lion King, complete with robotic lions and elephants, swinging monkeys and dancing zebras—all moving in sync with the movie soundtrack.

Visitors soak up the sights and sounds that have made Disneyland the world's most famous theme park. Snapshots with Mickey Mouse and Snow White. The "clip-clop" and "ding-ding" of horse-drawn trolleys. Red-vested vendors straining to stay earthbound under bouquets of balloons. The aroma of fresh popcorn and the giggles of enchanted children.

To put it simply, people come for the magic.

Maintaining that magic is an enormous task. The park in Anaheim, California, covers eighty-five acres, with an additional one hundred acres designated just for parking. It retains a staff of ten thousand employees—dubbed "cast members" by Walt Disney himself—which swells to twenty thousand during the peak summer season.

Providing millions of people with the time of their lives would drive most people goofy. How do cast members do it without feeling overwhelmed?

In a word, "T-E-A-M," says Gerry Aquino, Disneyland Ambassador and official host for the park. "That stands for 'Together Everyone Achieves Magic.'" The acronym, according to Aquino, applies to the whole staff, from popcorn sellers to ride operators to singers and dancers to the night crew that puts a fresh layer of luster on the park for the next day.

Aquino explains that Disneyland personnel are trained to see themselves as performers in a production rather than mere employees. "The production's success depends on individual performances," he explains. "Also, each cast member must see visitors as individuals. We consider each guest a VIP. The key to making the production work is to entertain people one at a time."[1]

Individuals doing their part to reach other individuals. When the mission of the Magic Kingdom is explained in those terms, it doesn't seem so overwhelming, does it?

The same is true in God's kingdom. Jesus told us, "Go therefore and make disciples of all the nations" (Matt. 28:19). That means taking the gospel to more than five billion people—a staggering project! But it can be accomplished when done person to person.

If you get tired just thinking about reaching the world for Christ, relax. You don't have to quit your job and become a traveling evangelist. You just need to share your faith naturally and sensitively—to one person at a time. Want to see this in action before trying it yourself? Then turn to Acts 8, and let's observe how the Great Commission unfolded in the life of Jesus' disciple Philip.

Philip's Background: From Persecution to Proclamation

In the first century, the seeds of the gospel were scattered by the winds of persecution. With Saul of Tarsus looking on, religious leaders stoned Stephen after his compelling—and convicting—sermon (Acts 7:52–60). Those stones sent ripples of persecution through Jerusalem, driving believers out to all of Judea and Samaria (8:1b). Did persecution dampen their spirits? No, just the opposite:

> Therefore, those who had been scattered went about preaching the word. (v. 4)

One of those scattered, preaching Christians was a man named Philip.

Philip's "Person-to-Person" Experience

Through Philip, God had stirred up the city of Samaria into a

---

1. From an interview with Gerry Aquino, Disneyland Ambassador, March 15, 1995, by Gary Matlack.

state of revival (8:5–13). When the apostles heard that he was up to his ears in new believers, they dispatched Peter and John to help him (vv. 14–25). How encouraging! Their ministry was burgeoning, and people were growing in the love of God. This would be a great place to settle down and nurture new believers, wouldn't it? Well, don't hammer down that tent peg so fast.

Right in the middle of this flourishing metropolitan ministry, the Lord uprooted Philip and set him on a desert road . . . to reach one person. Verses 26–39 record the experience, from which six key words emerge to help us share the gospel with people we encounter.

Sensitivity

> But an angel of the Lord spoke to Philip saying, "Arise and go south to the road that descends from Jerusalem to Gaza." (This is a desert road.) And he arose and went. (vv. 26–27a)

Oh, that we were all so sensitive to God's leading! Philip "arose and went" immediately after the angel directed him southward. No questions. No bargaining. No complaints about being pulled from city revival to wilderness witnessing. He just went.

What about us? Do we keep our spiritual sails unfurled, watching for them to flutter with a gust of God's wind? Or do we prefer to row along at our own speed, oblivious to the breeze? Through Scripture, circumstances, and inner promptings, the Holy Spirit will guide us. But reaching others for Christ requires that we stay sensitive to His leading, whether we're on a plane, in a classroom, in the office, or sitting in our neighbor's living room.

Availability

> And behold, there was an Ethiopian eunuch, a court official of Candace, queen of the Ethiopians, who was in charge of all her treasure; and he had come to Jerusalem to worship. And he was returning and sitting in his chariot, and was reading the prophet Isaiah. And the Spirit said to Philip, "Go up and join this chariot." (vv. 27b–29)

Availability and sensitivity are twins—with slight variations. Both entail openness to God's leading; but where *sensitivity* emphasizes the ears (listening to and initially responding to God), *availability* focuses more on the feet (moving them in whatever direction God specifies). Sensitivity says, "I hear You, Lord, and I'm on my way." Availability says, "OK, where's the next turn?" Once Philip left Samaria, he kept his eyes open for God's road signs.

The Spirit led him to a royal eunuch poring over the Scriptures in his chariot. Commentator Simon Kistemaker describes this traveler as "the chief treasurer. He has the prominent position of chancellor of the exchequer, or finance minister, in charge of the royal treasury and national revenue" of Ethiopia.[2] William Barclay sheds light on the purpose of the man's journey:

> This eunuch had been to Jerusalem to worship. In those days the world was full of people who were weary of the many gods and the loose morals of the nations. They came to Judaism and there found the one God and the austere moral standards which gave life meaning. If they accepted Judaism and were circumcised they were called *proselytes*; if they did not go that length but continued to attend the Jewish synagogues and to read the Jewish scriptures they were called *God-fearers* This Ethiopian must have been one of these searchers who came to rest in Judaism either as a proselyte or a God-fearer.[3]

So Philip, taking his directions from the Spirit of God, pulled up beside this inquisitive official.

Initiative

As he approached the chariot, Philip heard the familiar words of Isaiah 53 read contemplatively by the Ethiopian. What do you think was going through the evangelist's mind just then? "Oh, this is too good to be true—he's reading about the Messiah. OK, deep breaths, deep breaths. I've got him now. Just another minute and . . ." Not likely, judging from the text:

> And when Philip had run up, he heard him reading Isaiah the prophet, and said, "Do you understand what you are reading?" (v. 30)

2. Simon J. Kistemaker, *New Testament Commentary: Exposition of the Acts of the Apostles* (Grand Rapids, Mich.: Baker Book House, 1990), p. 312.

3. William Barclay, *The Acts of the Apostles*, rev. ed., The Daily Study Bible Series (Philadelphia, Pa.: Westminster Press, 1976), pp. 68–69.

Philip started with a simple, yet thoughtful, question—and waited for an answer. He took the initiative in the conversation, setting a tone that didn't try to impress or insult. He just asked a question. There's nothing like a good question to open people up and introduce the topic of spirituality. You might want to try some of these:

- "What do you think is wrong with the world today?"

- "Who do you think is the greatest person who ever lived?"

- "You know, there's a lot about the 'religious right' in the news today. I'm curious, what's your perception of Christianity?"

- "Do you find in your line of work that most people are honest and treat others fairly?"

Just remember, taking the initiative doesn't mean we have to bully people with our message. Truth and tact can come bundled in the same package.

Courtesy

The gospel of Christ isn't a box of chocolates. Not everyone who gets a taste will say, "What a treat. Can I have some more?" The message will offend many, simply because it makes clear distinctions between right and wrong (see Matt. 15:12; Rom. 9:33). We, however, don't have to add to the offense by *being offensive*. Philip treated the eunuch with respect, courtesy, and dignity. In answer to Philip's question, the eunuch responded:

> "Well, how could I, unless someone guides me?"
> And he invited Philip to come up and sit with him.
> Now the passage of Scripture which he was reading was this:
> "He was led as a sheep to slaughter;
> And as a lamb before its shearer is silent,
> So He does not open His mouth.
> In humiliation His judgment was taken
>   away;
> Who shall relate His generation?
> For His life is removed from the earth."
> And the eunuch answered Philip and said, "Please tell me, of whom does the prophet say this? Of himself, or of someone else?" (Acts 8:31–34)

Philip asked a question (v. 30) and waited for an answer. He listened. He was attentive. He waited to be invited into the chariot. And he lovingly led the eunuch through the pages of the Old Testament to Christ Himself (v. 35).

Our attitude and actions make a big difference in whether we're granted a hearing. Ironically, some Christians seem most un-Christlike when they're sharing His very words. We need to dispense with pushiness and pride and instead demonstrate Jesus' kindness and humility. Listen more. Judge less. Talk *with* people, not *at* them. Smile. Look the person in the eye. Offer a firm handshake.

By the way, there's nothing winsome about bad breath or body odor. The difference between repelling and attracting a non-Christian could be as simple as a breath mint or stick of deodorant.

Isn't it worth the effort to be tactful, courteous, and pleasant—considering how precious this unsaved person is to God?

Precision

Philip was not only courteous, he was also precise. That is, he kept the conversation focused on Christ.

> And Philip opened his mouth, and beginning from
> this Scripture he preached Jesus to him. (v. 35)

We think of preaching as speaking before a large crowd. Philip, however, "preached" to one person. Did he stand up, then, in the chariot and ask for a show of hands or deliver an altar call? No. The word for *preached* here can be translated simply "told him the good news" (NIV).

Starting with the eunuch's frame of reference, Isaiah 53, Philip shared the good news of Jesus Christ. He didn't debate various theories on when the book of Isaiah was written. He avoided badmouthing the synagogue for failing to declare Christ. He didn't present a survey of world religions. Nor did he condemn the eunuch for his employment in a pagan government. He simply shared Christ.

When we engage others in this kind of conversation, we need to understand that many are in the midst of inner distractions. Some may have been mistreated by Christians. Others are running from God, sending up smoke screens to avoid facing their predicament. Still others are downright antagonistic toward the faith. When such dynamics enter our discussions with nonbelievers, we must acknowledge their concerns but keep the spotlight on the death and resurrection of Jesus Christ.

Decisiveness

> And as they went along the road they came to some water; and the eunuch said, "Look! Water! What prevents me from being baptized?" And Philip said, "If you believe with all your heart, you may." And he answered and said, "I believe that Jesus Christ is the Son of God." And he ordered the chariot to stop; and they both went down into the water, Philip as well as the eunuch; and he baptized him. (Acts 8:36–38)

"Can I be baptized now?"

"Wait a minute," said Philip. "Do you believe what I've shared with you?"

Having presented the message, Philip helped the eunuch understand that following Christ involves making a clear decision.

A word of caution here. Some evangelism techniques emphasize "closing the sale." In other words, guiding people to the point of decision, getting them to pray the "sinner's prayer" before we leave them. But there are a couple of dangers in this kind of thinking.

If we make a "prayer of salvation" our goal, we might be tempted to manipulate the message to that end—making the gospel something it's not. Such an approach can also cause us to stop viewing the lost as real people with real needs. Instead, they become "targets," potential notches on our Bible.

We need to realize that our responsibility is to clearly communicate the message, not convert sinners. It is the Holy Spirit who draws people to Christ and provides the gift of eternal life.

When God does lead individuals to embrace the gospel during a conversation, as He did with the eunuch, we can help them understand their decision and get them started on the road to new life. Which is what Philip did. And the eunuch "went on his way rejoicing" (v. 39b), carrying the seeds of the gospel home to Africa.

"Make disciples of all the nations" doesn't sound so overwhelming once we realize that God is accomplishing His plan through each of us—one person at a time. In that sense, maybe the Disney song is right: "It's a small world after all."

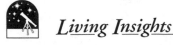

Greed did me in.

The caller had promised a free gift if I would allow a representative from her company to come by and give a short presentation on their home fire-alarm system. I didn't need an alarm system, of course. But for a freebie, I figured it was worth a listen.

So here I was, ninety minutes into a high-pressure harangue by two complete strangers. Under the watchful eye of his female superior, the associate gushed like an uncapped hydrant while fanning through a notebook full of statistics and photos of charred corpses who, naturally, didn't use his company's product. He interrupted his pitch only to ask an occasional question (he would use my answers against me later) or remind me how foolish it was for anyone to be without this device.

According to him, my home could spontaneously combust at any moment—maybe even in my sleep. Dust underneath the refrigerator. Faulty wiring behind outlets ("You just can't trust homebuilders"). An open field behind my home. I was doomed!

"No thanks," I said, when he took his first breath in an hour and a half. That's when the boss lady jumped in to close the sale. Then the real arm-twisting started.

"Are you serious?" she asked, incredulous that I could refuse in the face of such indisputable evidence.

"Sorry," I said. "It's not in the budget."

She kept pushing. So I got mad. And just before I threw them out of the house, she actually tried to recruit me to help sell her product. The nerve!

I felt cheap, used, manipulated. Like nothing more than a potential increase on their next commission check. I got my complimentary gift—an automatic appliance timer. But I would much rather have paid for it than endure such humiliation.

Believe it or not, that's how some Christians share the gospel. Like salespeople before a captive customer, they go for the jugular, determined to do whatever is necessary to sell "fire insurance." And if the listener dares to reject the gospel, the coercion starts.

We don't see Jesus doing that in the Scriptures. Or Peter. Or Paul. They delivered the truth with boldness and confidence—convinced they had the right "product." But there was no arm-twisting. No modifying the gospel so more people would buy it. They shared, discussed, listened. They allowed people the freedom to accept the gospel or reject it. They spread the Word, but left the results to God.

We need to acknowledge the power and providence of God more in evangelism. We don't move hearts to the point of belief. He does. We're simply part of the process. So let's be diligent. Let's get the message out. Let's be sensitive to opportunities and clear in our presentation. But let's leave the saving to God. When He closes a sale, He guarantees it . . . forever.

 Living Insights STUDY TWO

This brings us to the end of our study. What discoveries did you make along the way? Did you unroll a new blueprint for marriage, perhaps? Or see employment from a fresh perspective? Or find the lost gem of worship? Write down the major discoveries you made in each chapter.

Discovering How to Make a Marriage Work _____

_____

_____

_____

Discovering the Value of Deep Friendships _____

_____

_____

_____

Discovering That a Job Isn't Just a Job _____

_____

_____

_____

Discovering the Missing Jewel of Worship _____

_____

Discovering the Difference between God's Ways and Our Ways

_____

_____

_____

_____

Discovering Your Part in Reaching the Lost _____

_____

_____

_____

Thanks for joining us. And remember, God's Word is full of new discoveries for those who keep looking.

BOOKS FOR PROBING FURTHER

W e're never too old, too experienced, or too "spiritual" to make new discoveries because the riches of God's Word can never be exhausted. So if you want to dig deeper into the topics we've covered in this guide, the following books will help.

Marriage

Harley, Willard F., Jr. *His Needs, Her Needs*. Old Tappan, N.J.: Fleming H. Revell Co., 1986.

Hendricks, Howard and Jeanne, gen. eds., with LaVonne Neff. *Husbands and Wives*. Wheaton, Ill.: Scripture Press Publications, Victor Books, 1988.

Swindoll, Charles R. *Strike the Original Match*. Portland, Oreg.: Multnomah Press, 1980.

Friendship

McGinnis, Alan Loy. *The Friendship Factor*. Minneapolis, Minn.: Augsburg Publishing House, 1979.

Career

Hart, Archibald D. *The Crazy-Making Workplace*. Ann Arbor, Mich.: Servant Publications, Vine Books, 1993.

Miller, Arthur F., and Ralph T. Mattson. *The Truth about You: Discover What You Should Be Doing with Your Life*. Old Tappan, N.J.: Fleming H. Revell Co., 1977.

Sherman, Doug, and William Hendricks. *Your Work Matters to God*. Colorado Springs, Colo.: NavPress, 1987.

Worship

Allen, Ronald, and Gordon Borror. *Worship: Rediscovering the Missing Jewel*. Portland, Oreg.: Multnomah Press, 1982.

Ortlund, Anne. *Up with Worship: How to Quit Playing Church.* Revised edition. Ventura, Calif.: Gospel Light Publications, Regal Books, 1982.

Sproul, R. C. *The Holiness of God.* Wheaton, Ill.: Tyndale House Publishers, Living Books, 1985.

Tozer, A. W. *Whatever Happened to Worship?* Comp. and ed. Gerald B. Smith. Camp Hill, Pa.: Christian Publications, 1985.

God's Ways

Basinger, David and Randall, eds. *Predestination and Free Will.* Downers Grove, Ill.: InterVarsity Press, 1986.

Friesen, Garry, with J. Robin Maxson. *Decision Making and the Will of God.* Portland, Oreg.: Multnomah Press, 1980.

Piper, John. *Desiring God: Meditations of a Christian Hedonist.* Portland, Oreg.: Multnomah Press, 1986.

Evangelism

Aldrich, Joseph C. *Gentle Persuasion: Creative Ways to Introduce Your Friends to Christ.* Portland, Oreg.: Multnomah Press, 1988.

————. *Life-Style Evangelism: Crossing Traditional Boundaries to Reach the Unbelieving World.* Portland, Oreg.: Multnomah Press, 1981.

Little, Paul E. *How to Give Away Your Faith.* Downers Grove, Ill.: InterVarsity Press, 1966.

Petersen, Jim. *Living Proof.* Colorado Springs, Colo.: NavPress, 1989. Originally published as *Evangelism as a Lifestyle,* 1980; and *Evangelism for Our Generation,* 1985.

Some of these books may be out of print and available only through a library. For those currently available, please contact your local Christian bookstore. Books by Charles R. Swindoll may be obtained through Insight for Living. IFL also offers some books by other authors—please note the ordering information that follows and contact the office that serves you.

ORDERING INFORMATION

MAKING NEW DISCOVERIES
Cassette Tapes and Study Guide

This Bible study guide was designed to be used independently or in conjunction with the broadcast of Chuck Swindoll's taped messages which are listed below. If you would like to order cassette tapes or further copies of this study guide, please see the information given below and the order forms provided at the end of this guide.

		U.S.	Canada
MND	Study guide	$ 3.95 ea.	$ 5.25 ea.
MNDCS	Cassette series, includes all individual tapes, album cover, and one complimentary study guide	22.00	24.50
MND 1–3	Individual cassettes, includes messages A and B	6.00 ea.	7.48 ea.

The prices are subject to change without notice.

MND 1–A: *Discovering How to Make a Marriage Work*— Genesis 2:24–25; Proverbs 24:3–4
   B: *Discovering the Value of Deep Friendships*— Ecclesiastes 4:9–12; John 15:12–17

MND 2–A: *Discovering That a Job Isn't Just a Job*— Selected Scriptures
   B: *Discovering the Missing Jewel of Worship*—Isaiah 6:1–8

MND 3–A: *Discovering the Difference between God's Ways and Our Ways*—Genesis 45:1–8; 50:18–21; Romans 8:28–32
   B: *Discovering Your Part in Reaching the Lost**— Acts 8:25–40

*This message was not a part of the original series but is compatible with it.

How to Order by Phone or FAX
(Credit card orders only)

United States: 1-800-772-8888 from 7:00 A.M. to 4:30 P.M., Pacific time, Monday through Friday
FAX (714) 575-5496 anytime, day or night

61

Canada: 1-800-663-7639, Vancouver residents call (604) 596-2910 from 8:00 A.M. to 5:00 P.M., Pacific time, Monday through Friday FAX (604) 596-2975 anytime, day or night

Australia and the South Pacific: (03) 9-872-4606 or FAX (03) 9-874-8890 from 8:00 A.M. to 5:00 P.M., Monday through Friday

Other International Locations: call the Ordering Services Department in the United States at (714) 575-5000 during the hours listed above.

How to Order by Mail

United States
- Mail to: Processing Services Department
  Insight for Living
  Post Office Box 69000
  Anaheim, CA 92817-0900
- Sales tax: California residents add 7.25%.
- Shipping and handling charges must be added to each order. See chart on order form for amount.
- Payment: personal checks, money orders, credit cards (Visa, Master-Card, Discover Card, and American Express). No invoices or COD orders available.
- $10 fee for *any* returned check.

Canada
- Mail to: Insight for Living Ministries
  Post Office Box 2510
  Vancouver, BC V6B 3W7
- Sales tax: please add 7% GST. British Columbia residents also add 7% sales tax (on tapes or cassette series).
- Shipping and handling charges must be added to each order. See chart on order form for amount.
- Payment: personal cheques, money orders, credit cards (Visa, Master-Card). No invoices or COD orders available.
- Delivery: approximately four weeks.

Australia and the South Pacific
- Mail to: Insight for Living, Inc.
  GPO Box 2823 EE
  Melbourne, Victoria 3001, Australia
- Shipping: add 25% to the total order.

- Delivery: approximately four to six weeks.
- Payment: personal checks payable in Australian funds, international money orders, or credit cards (Visa, MasterCard, and BankCard).

Other International Locations
- Mail to: Processing Services Department
  Insight for Living
  Post Office Box 69000
  Anaheim, CA 92817-0900
- Shipping and delivery time: please see chart that follows.
- Payment: personal checks payable in U.S. funds, international money orders, or credit cards (Visa, MasterCard, and American Express).

Type of Shipping	Postage Cost	Delivery
Surface	10% of total order*	6 to 10 weeks
Airmail	25% of total order*	under 6 weeks

*Use U.S. price as a base.

Our Guarantee

Your complete satisfaction is our top priority here at Insight for Living. If you're not completely satisfied with anything you order, please return it for full credit, a refund, or a replacement, as *you* prefer.

Insight for Living Catalog

The Insight for Living catalog features study guides, tapes, and books by a variety of Christian authors. To obtain a free copy, call us at the numbers listed above.

Order Form
United States, Australia, and Other International Locations
(Canadian residents please use order form on reverse side.)

MNDCS represents the entire *Making New Discoveries* series in a special album cover, while MND 1–3 are the individual tapes included in the series. MND represents this study guide, should you desire to order additional copies.

MND	Study guide	$ 3.95 ea.
MNDCS	Cassette series, includes all individual tapes, album cover, and one complimentary study guide	22.00
MND 1–3	Individual cassettes, includes messages A and B	6.00 ea.

Product Code	Product Description	Quantity	Unit Price	Total
			$	$

			Subtotal
			California Residents—Sales Tax Add 7.25% of subtotal.
Amount of Order	First Class	UPS	UPS ❏ First Class ❏
$10.00 and under	1.50	4.25	Shipping and handling must be added. See chart for charges.
$10.01 to 35.00	3.50	4.50	
$35.01 to 50.00	4.50	4.75	Non-United States Residents Australia add 25%. All other
$50.00 and over	5.55	5.25	locations: U.S. price plus 10% surface postage or 25% airmail.

Fed Ex and Fourth Class are also available. Please call for details.

Gift to Insight for Living *Tax-deductible in the United States.*	
Total Amount Due *Please do not send cash.*	$

Prices are subject to change without notice.

Payment by: ❏ Check or money order payable to Insight for Living ❏ Credit card

(Circle one):   Visa   MasterCard   Discover Card   American Express   BankCard
(In Australia)

Number _____

Expiration Date _____   Signature _____
We cannot process your credit card purchase without your signature.

Name _____

Address _____

City _____   State _____

Zip Code _____   Country _____

Telephone (____) _____   Radio Station ____ ____ ____ ____
If questions arise concerning your order, we may need to contact you.

Mail this order form to the Processing Services Department at one of these addresses:

Insight for Living
Post Office Box 69000, Anaheim, CA 92817-0900

Insight for Living, Inc.
GPO Box 2823 EE, Melbourne, VIC 3001, Australia

Order Form
Canadian Residents
(Residents of the United States, Australia, and other international locations, please use order form on reverse side.)

MNDCS represents the entire *Making New Discoveries* series in a special album cover, while MND 1–3 are the individual tapes included in the series. MND represents this study guide, should you desire to order additional copies.

MND	Study guide	$ 5.25 ea.
MNDCS	Cassette series,	24.50
	includes all individual tapes, album cover, and one complimentary study guide	
MND 1–3	Individual cassettes,	7.48 ea.
	includes messages A and B	

Product Code	Product Description	Quantity	Unit Price	Total
			$	$

Amount of Order	Canada Post
Orders to $10.00	2.00
$10.01 to 30.00	3.50
$30.01 to 50.00	5.00
$50.01 to 99.99	7.00
$100 and over	Free

Loomis is also available. Please call for details.

Subtotal	
Add 7% GST	
British Columbia Residents Add 7% sales tax on individual tapes or cassette series.	
Shipping Shipping and handling must be added. See chart for charges.	
Gift to Insight for Living Ministries Tax-deductible in Canada.	
Total Amount Due Please do not send cash.	$

Prices are subject to change without notice.

Payment by: ❑ Cheque or money order payable to Insight for Living Ministries
❑ Credit card

(Circle one): Visa   MasterCard   Number _____

Expiration Date _____   Signature _____
We cannot process your credit card purchase without your signature.

Name _____

Address _____

City _____   Province _____

Postal Code _____   Country _____

Telephone (___) _____   Radio Station ___ ___ ___ ___
If questions arise concerning your order, we may need to contact you.

Mail this order form to the Processing Services Department at the following address:

Insight for Living Ministries
Post Office Box 2510
Vancouver, BC, Canada V6B 3W7

Order Form
United States, Australia, and Other International Locations
(Canadian residents please use order form on reverse side.)

MNDCS represents the entire *Making New Discoveries* series in a special album cover, while MND 1–3 are the individual tapes included in the series. MND represents this study guide, should you desire to order additional copies.

MND	Study guide	$ 3.95 ea.
MNDCS	Cassette series,	22.00
	includes all individual tapes, album cover, and one complimentary study guide	
MND 1–3	Individual cassettes, includes messages A and B	6.00 ea.

Product Code	Product Description	Quantity	Unit Price	Total
			$	$

Amount of Order	First Class	UPS	
			Subtotal
			California Residents—Sales Tax Add 7.25% of subtotal.
$10.00 and under	1.50	4.25	**UPS ❑ First Class ❑** Shipping and handling must be added. See chart for charges.
$10.01 to 35.00	3.50	4.50	
$35.01 to 50.00	4.50	4.75	**Non-United States Residents** Australia add 25%. All other locations: U.S. price plus 10% surface postage or 25% airmail.
$50.00 and over	5.55	5.25	

Fed Ex and Fourth Class are also available. Please call for details.

Gift to Insight for Living Tax-deductible in the United States.

Total Amount Due Please do not send cash. $

Prices are subject to change without notice.

Payment by: ❑ Check or money order payable to Insight for Living   ❑ Credit card
(Circle one):   Visa   MasterCard   Discover Card   American Express   BankCard (In Australia)

Number _____

Expiration Date _____   Signature _____
We cannot process your credit card purchase without your signature.

Name _____

Address _____

City _____   State _____

Zip Code _____   Country _____

Telephone (____) _____   Radio Station ____ ____ ____ ____
If questions arise concerning your order, we may need to contact you.

Mail this order form to the Processing Services Department at one of these addresses:

Insight for Living
Post Office Box 69000, Anaheim, CA 92817-0900

Insight for Living, Inc.
GPO Box 2823 EE, Melbourne, VIC 3001, Australia

Order Form
Canadian Residents

(Residents of the United States, Australia, and other international locations, please use order form on reverse side.)

MNDCS represents the entire *Making New Discoveries* series in a special album cover, while MND 1–3 are the individual tapes included in the series. MND represents this study guide, should you desire to order additional copies.

MND	Study guide	$ 5.25 ea.
MNDCS	Cassette series,	24.50
	includes all individual tapes, album cover, and one complimentary study guide	
MND 1–3	Individual cassettes,	7.48 ea.
	includes messages A and B	

Product Code	Product Description	Quantity	Unit Price	Total
			$	$

Amount of Order	Canada Post
Orders to $10.00	2.00
$10.01 to 30.00	3.50
$30.01 to 50.00	5.00
$50.01 to 99.99	7.00
$100 and over	Free

Loomis is also available. Please call for details.

Subtotal	
Add 7% GST	
British Columbia Residents *Add 7% sales tax on individual tapes or cassette series.*	
Shipping *Shipping and handling must be added. See chart for charges.*	
Gift to Insight for Living Ministries *Tax-deductible in Canada.*	
Total Amount Due *Please do not send cash.*	$

Prices are subject to change without notice.

Payment by: ❑ Cheque or money order payable to Insight for Living Ministries
❑ Credit card

(Circle one): Visa   MasterCard   Number _____

Expiration Date _____   Signature _____

We cannot process your credit card purchase without your signature.

Name _____

Address _____

City _____ Province _____

Postal Code _____ Country _____

Telephone (___) _____ Radio Station ____ ____ ____ ____

If questions arise concerning your order, we may need to contact you.

Mail this order form to the Processing Services Department at the following address:

Insight for Living Ministries
Post Office Box 2510
Vancouver, BC, Canada V6B 3W7